SCOTTIE BOOKS

# THE ROMANS IN SCOTLAND

ACTIVITY BOOK

By Frances Jarvie

Illustrated by Carrie Philip

Edinburgh : HMSO
National Museums of Scotland

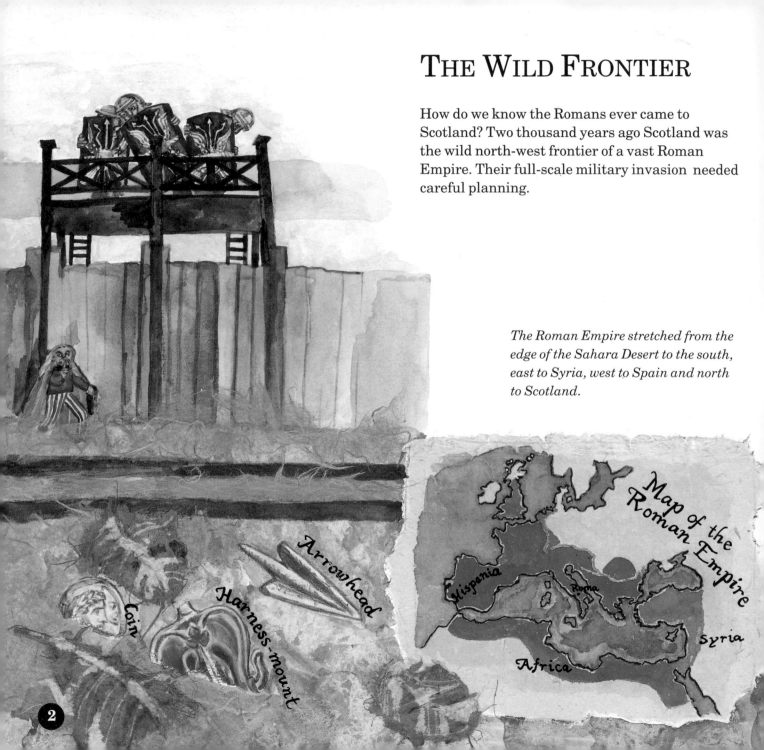

# THE WILD FRONTIER

How do we know the Romans ever came to Scotland? Two thousand years ago Scotland was the wild north-west frontier of a vast Roman Empire. Their full-scale military invasion needed careful planning.

*The Roman Empire stretched from the edge of the Sahara Desert to the south, east to Syria, west to Spain and north to Scotland.*

Map of the Roman Empire

Hispania

Roma

Syria

Africa

Coin

Harness-mount

Arrowhead

Roads were built for the advancing troops. Forts, watchtowers, camps and supplies had to be provided for the soldiers. Two awesome walls were built to contain the Celts. Emperor Hadrian ordered a wall between the rivers Solway and Tyne and Emperor Antoninus had a further wall built between the rivers Clyde and Forth. From these military wonders archaeologists can now tell us how the Roman army lived at the most northerly edge of their empire.

Yet despite these plans, the Roman army never conquered Scotland. The Celtic tribes were experts at guerrilla warfare. We do not have in Scotland the remains of the fine towns built in the south of England. But we do have Scotland's first written history. A Roman historian, Tacitus, wrote about Agricola – the Roman general who invaded Scotland in AD 80.

TRIMONTIUM NEEDS
**YOU**

Sign on as a Trooper at Trimontium. Vacancies for all ranks. (see page 40).

Roman parade helmet found at Newstead

Who can tell? You might be the next person to uncover a stretch of Roman road or find a Roman coin. The past is often like a jigsaw awaiting the missing pieces!

3

# THE CELTS

The tribes in Caledonia, as the Romans called Scotland, were Celtic peoples. They spoke a language like Gaelic and were clever at making tools and weapons from bronze and iron, as well as beautiful jewellery from gold, silver and bronze.

The Celts were good farmers who grew crops and kept cattle, pigs and sheep. They also hunted deer and wild boar. They admired the boar as it was so fierce.

Both men and women had long hair, often plaited. The men had long moustaches, wore trousers and had long tunics with a cloak over the top. Feasting and fighting were favourite pastimes. After a battle they would feast for days on end, telling stories, singing, reciting poems and drinking too much! The best warriors were rewarded with the 'hero's portion', often the thigh of roast boar.

Their homes varied according to where they lived. A wooden roundhouse was popular in lowland areas, made from timber and interwoven branches plastered with clay.

In some places houses called crannogs were built on platforms in lochs or bogs. To the far north were the brochs – small, round, stone forts, only found in Scotland. On hill-tops they built forts, such as Traprain Law in East Lothian.

The Romans traded with some of the Celts for foodstuffs as they had a hungry army to feed. In exchange the Celts were given Roman pottery, glass and ornaments.

The Roman Legion XX Valeria Victrix used a charging boar on it's legions badge. The boar was the main sacred beast of the Celts.

Oh Yes! What a Boar

*The Celts designed interlaced patterns – often of animals. Look at these symmetrical patterns. Can you copy any of them? Now try designing some of your own.*

Oh No What a bore!

Spot the Wild Boar

How many wild boars can you spot in the pages of this book?

(Answer on page 40.)

5

# THE ROMAN ARMY IN SCOTLAND

*Horn Player*

Scotland was the main military zone of Roman Britain. Units from Germany, Belgium, France, Yugoslavia and Syria all served in the country. Latin was the language of the army, but these troops also used their native languages. New recruits were drawn from the local people where the unit was stationed.

*Flag Standard Bearer*

*Legionary*

*Auxiliar*

*Signifer*

**Flag standard bearer**
*Roman helmets were like modern crash helmets. Made of bronze, padded inside, and with neck and ear flaps to protect faces from sword cuts.*

**Horn player**
*The cornu was like a French horn, used for making trumpet calls in camp and for playing tunes on the march.*

**Signifer - standard bearer**
*Each century had its own standard. It was a wooden pole decorated with medals and wreaths awarded for bravery in battle. He wore a bearskin (or wolf or lion) over his helmet.*

**Legionary**
*A Roman citizen. He signed on for 25 years and could rise to the rank of centurion.*

**Auxiliary**
*Enlisted from the provinces. Made a Roman citizen after 25 years' service. Infantryman or cavalryman, belonged to a unit of either 500 or 1000.*

There was a lot of contact between the army and the tribes in Caledonia – not much of the soldiers' time was spent actually fighting. Civil settlements grew up outside the forts – for example at Inveresk, Cramond and Carriden. Roman soldiers were not allowed to marry during military service but many had children to local women or slaves and brought up their families as best they could.

Off-duty soldiers enjoyed racing, wrestling, throwing games, hunting and fishing. They also loved gambling and playing draughts.

Order in the army was strictly enforced. If soldiers deserted or refused to obey orders, the penalty was death. Other punishments were extra duties, reduced rations or loss of pay. The Roman army was a highly organised and very successful war machine even at the farthest outpost of the empire.

**Optio**
*Second in command to the Centurion.*
**Centurion**
*In charge of a unit of 80 men. His helmet has a crest running from side to side. Greaves (shinguards) protect his legs. His shield is made from wood in thin layers, covered with tough leather.*

Centurion

Optio

YIKES!

JOIN the ROMAN ARMY
Make your own Roman helmet
Prob Busin using gold and silver card

I. card strips

II. pasted paper strips

III. back peak front peak

IV. Glue together back peak front side flaps

7

# Battle of Mons Graupius

One of the biggest battles in Scotland against the Romans is thought to have taken place on the slopes of Bennachie - 20 miles north east of Aberdeen.

Each army had different types of weapons and ways of fighting. This decided who won and lost the battle in AD 84.

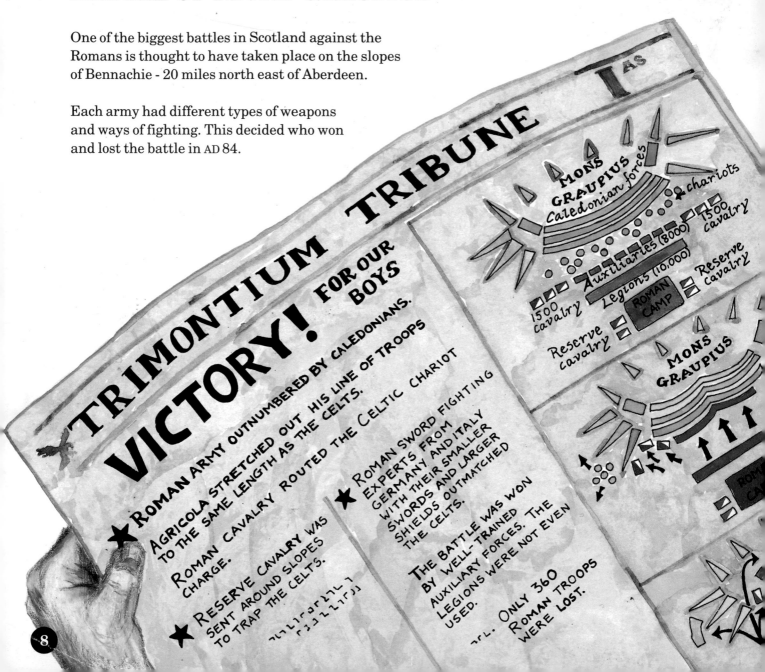

## TRIMONTIUM TRIBUNE

## VICTORY! FOR OUR BOYS

★ ROMAN ARMY OUTNUMBERED BY CALEDONIANS.

AGRICOLA STRETCHED OUT HIS LINE OF TROOPS TO THE SAME LENGTH AS THE CELTS.

ROMAN CAVALRY ROUTED THE CELTIC CHARIOT CHARGE.

★ RESERVE CAVALRY WAS SENT AROUND SLOPES TO TRAP THE CELTS.

ROMAN SWORD FIGHTING EXPERTS FROM GERMANY AND ITALY WITH THEIR SMALLER SWORDS AND LARGER SHIELDS OUTMATCHED THE CELTS.

★ THE BATTLE WAS WON BY WELL-TRAINED AUXILIARY FORCES. THE LEGIONS WERE NOT EVEN USED.

ONLY 360 ROMAN TROOPS WERE LOST.

MONS GRAUPIUS
Caledonian forces
chariots
1500 cavalry
Auxiliaries (8000)
Legions (10,000)
ROMAN CAMP
Reserve cavalry
1500 cavalry
Reserve cavalry

MONS GRAUPIUS
ROMAN CAMP

# The Celtic Clarion

## The Killing Fields: A Nation mourns
### One out of every three Celts killed. Calgacus crushed

■ 30,000 CALEDONIAN FORCES UNDER THE LEADERSHIP OF CALGACUS WERE PLACED ON THE HILLSIDE FACING THE ROMAN CAMP. CHARIOTS WERE PLACED IN FRONT OF THE TROOPS.

■ CHARIOT CHARGE NO MATCH FOR FASTER ROMAN CAVALRY.

THE CELTIC WARRIORS HAD LONG, HEAVY SWORDS AND SMALL SHIELDS. THE DESIGNS ON THE SHIELDS WERE MEANT TO GIVE THEM MAGICAL PROTECTION IN BATTLE. THE CHARIOTEER'S JOB WAS TO DRIVE TWO FAST PONIES AT FULL SPEED THROUGH THE ENEMY RANKS. THE WARRIOR'S JOB WAS TO SLICE OFF AS MANY HEADS AS POSSIBLE.

■ VOLLEYS OF SPEARS AND JAVELINS EXCHANGED FOLLOWED BY HAND-TO-HAND FIGHTING.

■ CELTS HAD TO RETREAT UPHILL OVER PILES OF DEAD AND WOUNDED. RESERVES WERE ORDERED TO ATTACK ROMAN TROOPS AT THE REAR BUT WERE SCATTERED BY AGRICOLA'S CAVALRY.

*Facing the music!* The Celtic war trumpet, or carnyx was used in battle to terrify the enemy. The head was in the shape of a wild boar and you could get the scream of a pig from the way the horn was blown.

*Find out about the didgeridoo. Like the carnyx this Aboriginal instrument has no holes or valves - the sound depends on the way it is played.*

ROMAN CAMP

**9**

# TRIMONTIUM (NEWSTEAD) — A ROMAN FORT

Trimontium – the place of the three peaks – was the Roman military headquarters in the south of Scotland. It was at the centre of the Roman road network in the country. Distances were worked out from Trimontium.

The fort was built on a mound overlooking the River Tweed, so it was in a key position. Sadly none of the fort can be seen today, but the Trimontium exhibition in Melrose has a wonderful display of fort life and is well worth a visit. (Details on page 40)

**A TRICKY ONE!**

Which of these words are the odd ones out?

triangle
tricycle
triplets
triple
tripod
trio
trinity
trilogy
trigger
tricolour

STANDARD FORT KIT No. II

### Drill Hall
Used for training men and horses. Training was hard. Men had to practise for hours learning how to handle swords and javelins.

### Principia
This was the H.Q. building with offices, a shrine and pillared courtyards. The standard of the garrison was kept safe here, was the pay chest kept in a strong room.

*(Answers on page 40)*

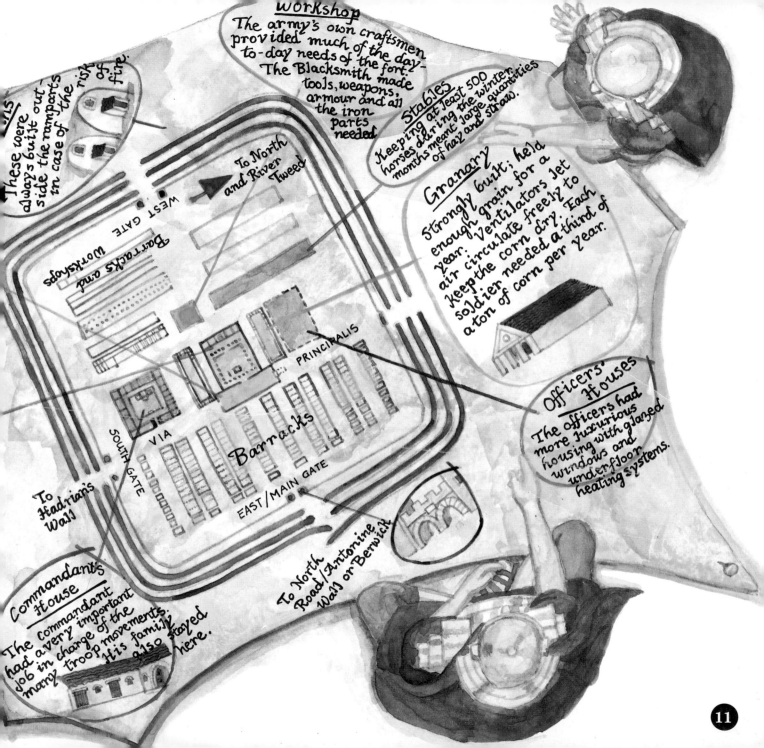

## Workshop
The army's own craftsmen provided much of the day-to-day needs of the fort. The Blacksmith made tools, weapons, armour and all the iron parts needed.

These were always built outside the ramparts in case of the risk of fire.

To North and River Tweed

WEST GATE

Barracks and Workshops

## Stables
Keeping at least 500 horses during the winter months meant large quantities of hay and straw.

## Granary
Strongly built; held enough grain for a year. Ventilators let air circulate freely to keep the corn dry. Each soldier needed a third of a ton of corn per year.

PRINCIPALIS

VIA

SOUTH GATE

Barracks

To Hadrian's Wall

EAST/MAIN GATE

## Officers' Houses
The officers had more luxurious housing with glazed windows and underfloor heating systems.

To North Antonine Road/Antonine Wall or Berwick

## Commandant's House
The commandant had a very important job in charge of the many troop movements. His family also stayed here.

**11**

# ROMAN SHIPS

After the Battle of Mons Graupius some of Agricola's ships were first to sail around Scotland, proving Britain was an island. It was then possible to work out the shape of Britain from the sailing times taken to go around our coastline.

When Agricola was ordered to advance north of the River Tay in AD 83, he used his fleet to torment the Celts. It was easier to use ships for carrying supplies than taking them across mountains, moors and bogs.

Ships were also useful for transporting the huge amount of supplies needed for the army in Scotland. Cramond on the Forth had a harbour and large stores for Agricola's troops. Much careful planning went into how to feed the troops. As the Roman generals knew too well – a hungry army is a useless army!

In peaceful times the merchant ships were used for trading. Crofters in the Hebrides may have traded their woollen cloth for Roman pottery and glassware.

## Roman merchant ship

Merchant ships were wider and heavier than the galleys. They were built to carry large cargoes of grain as well as goods from all over the Roman Empire to Britain.

Sails were used and it was steered by two huge paddles at the stern. Oars were used only when there was no wind. Ships like these would have reached the Orkney Islands and the Hebrides.

## Roman warship

Their warships were long, thin and fast. They were designed for the calmer waters of the Mediterranean rather than the stormier seas around Scotland. (Julius Caesar had to go back to the drawing board and have his transport fleet redesigned after his first invasion of Britain failed.) The warship, or galley, had a square sail and rows of oars on each side pulled by slaves or prisoners.

On the prow was a ramming device which could pierce the hull of an enemy ship and sink it. It could also move quickly against enemy ships and break their oars. They pulled in their own oars quickly just before hitting the ship.

Who pays the Ferryman?

When a Roman citizen died, a coin was often placed in their mouth. This was to pay for the boatman who would ferry them to their afterlife – across the River Styx to Hades, the underworld.

Roman Warship

Merchant Ship

Oceanus Atlanticus

PTOLEMY'S MAP of SCOTLAND

Caledonii

Vacomagi

Taezali

Venicones

Oceanus Germanicus

Oceanus Hibernicus

Ptolemy was an Egyptian geographer and astronomer who lived from AD 90 to AD 168. On his map of Scotland he wrote down the names of the native tribes in Roman Britain.

Check your atlas. What do we call these seas today?

(Answers on page 40.)

13

# HADRIAN'S WALL

*'We are the scum and scrapings of the empire. They tipped out the garbage-bin of the Eagles to make us what we are.'*
*(From* Frontier Wolf *by Rosemary Sutcliff)*

A posting to the boundary of Caledonia and beyond often served as a form of punishment for Roman soldiers. Our harsh climate, difficult terrain and constant threats from warring Celtic tribes were bad enough. But years of tough construction work also lay ahead.

In AD 122 Emperor Hadrian visited Britain and ordered his generals to build a wall, 73 miles long, to stretch from the Solway Firth to the River Tyne. As travellers had passed on stories to Rome of the Great Wall of China, built 200 years earlier, Hadrian perhaps decided to copy this idea.

He may have wanted to impress the native tribes with the power of Rome, as well as give the army useful work to do by keeping the peaceful part of Britain safe. So it was probably planned as a boundary between the tamed tribes to the south and the wild folks in Caledonia.

The wall was built in 5-mile stretches and along that section were 17 forts. At every mile between the forts were smaller forts called milecastles. Between the milecastles were signal turrets. All of these were manned by regiments of auxiliary soldiers. You can see replica sections of Hadrian's Wall at Vindolanda. Find out about fort life at Carvoran and see outstanding exhibitions at both sites. (Details on page 40)

4 million tonnes of stone were used
It stretched for 80 Roman miles.

The Wall was so solidly built that large sections of it still remain and can be seen today.

milecastle

Look carefully at the picture of the milecastle. Make a model of one using Lego or boxes, painted to show the stonework.

It was the 2nd, 6th and 20th Legions who were the craftsmen of the Wall. These legionaries were skilled in every possible trade – from builders and surveyors, to architects and stonemasons. The same legions toiled 20 years later to build the Antonine Wall further north.

Sons followed their fathers into guarding the Wall.

It took nearly 15 years to build. 18 000 soldiers worked on it.

There was a regiment of archers from Syria stationed at the Carvoran garrison.

# GODS AND GODDESSES

The Romans brought their own religion with them to Britain. Soldiers worshipped the traditional gods of Rome, Greece and Persia. Mithras was from ancient Iran, and from him came the Mithraic religion which was popular in the army. Mithras was seen as a kindly god who came between man and other gods. He is said to have killed a huge bull whose blood then gave life to all the crops.

From the rest of its body came all the plants of the earth. Followers of Mithras had to be brave and pass seven tests of hardship. After each test further mysteries of the religion were then revealed.

Soldiers built small shrines outside their forts and placed statues in them. Mars, god of war, and Minerva, goddess of wisdom, were popular with soldiers, as well as the native Celtic gods.

Mithras

Bacch

Janus (beginnings - depicted with two faces, one looking forward, one back)

Vesta

Jupiter (thunder and lightning, head of the Roman gods)

The circular temple at Carron Falkirk. It was demolished in 1743. known as Arthur's Oven.

A temple to Victory in a circular, beehive shape was built close to the fort at Falkirk on the Antonine Wall. The distance-slabs built for the Wall often showed Roman gods and goddesses. Soldiers also had to worship their emperor. This was to prove that they were loyal to him. When soldiers died on active service they were cremated. Their ashes were put in a stone-lined box, glass jar or pot. These were then buried in a cemetery outside the fort.

During the 4th century AD, Christianity began to take the place of the old gods. Tombstones show that the new religion began to spread into the army. As Christianity spread throughout the Roman world, it eventually became the official religion.

The first monastery in Scotland was set up by Ninian around AD 400 at Whithorn in Galloway. The monks trained there, then spread Christianity in southern Scotland.

*Aphrodite, the goddess of love, on Roman silver found at Traprain Law, East Lothian.*

*Find a picture of a Roman god or goddess and decorate a paper plate. Design a mosaic border around the edge. You could make a place mat to match your plate.*

*(Answers on page 40.)*

Diana (moon and hunting)

PICTURE QUIZ

Can you match the names to the gods and goddesses?

**17**

# THE ANTONINE WALL

As the Romans extended their empire northwards again, a new frontier, north of Hadrian's Wall, was built about AD 142 in the region of Antoninus Pius. It stretched for 37 miles, from Old Kilpatrick on the Clyde to Bridgeness on the Forth.

Unlike Hadrian's Wall, which was built of stone, the Antonine Wall had only a stone base, with turf blocks and a wooden battlement on top. A broad ditch was dug on the north side, and on the south side there was a road, the Military Way, linking up the 19 forts along the Wall.

You can still see sections of the Wall base in the New Kilpatrick Cemetery in Bearsden. The Romans chose such a good route that the same line was taken by the Forth and Clyde Canal, as well as the Glasgow – Edinburgh railway, many hundreds of years later.

Most of the work of building this new wall fell to the legions based in Britain in Antoninus's reign. The 2nd Legion, based at Caerleon in South Wales, the 6th and 20th based at York and Chester, all worked on the Wall. While working, they lived in large temporary camps.

Records of their work in the form of stone distance-slabs are unique – nothing similar has been found elsewhere in the Roman world.

When the Romans retreated from the Wall, the legionaries buried the slabs, so many are still waiting to be unearthed. You can see a display of them at the Hunterian Museum in Glasgow.

The Bridgeness slab was found in 1868 by a gardener. It is the largest found and marked the eastern end of the Wall. You can see it at the Museum of Antiquities in Edinburgh.

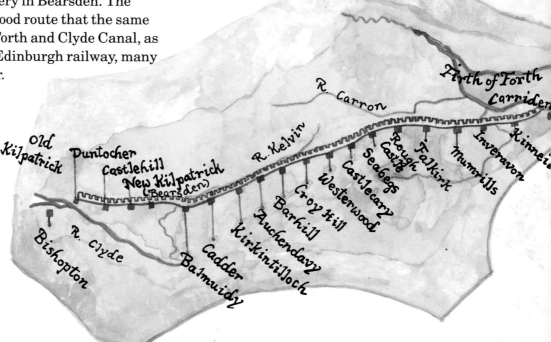

## The Bridgeness Slab

*To the left a Roman cavalryman aims his spear at naked tribesmen. To the right is an arch above legionary officers who are watching three animals being sacrificed at an altar.*

*Which animals are they?*
*(Answers on page 40.)*

IMP·CAES·TITO·AELIO
HADRIANTONINO
AVG·PIO·P·P·LEG·II
AVG·PER·M·P·IIIID·CLII
FEC

CHECK OUT YOUR ROMAN NUMERALS

Before playing this game

Throw a III to start

Take on more food from Invaresk - restart at I

Visit Vindolanda - miss a turn

Finish

TRIMON

Start

If you throw a II go for weapons practice

HILL

Spend the day at the Bearsden bath house - miss a turn to continue

Weapons practice - miss a turn

Intorese! reverboy

Attacked by pirates - miss a turn

**A Game for 2–4 players**

Use different coloured counters, buttons, or coins, for each player. Each throws the dice.

The highest scorer wins.

Start at Trimontium and race your opponents around Caledonia.

Avoid the hazards if you can!

# Amazing Facts

The Warwick Vase in the Burrell Collection, Glasgow, was reconstructed from pieces found in a lake by Hadrian's Villa, near Rome. Sir William Hamilton, a Scottish diplomat, who was interested in Roman antiquities, found them in 1770 after draining the lake. The vase is enormous — almost 3 metres in height — and is made of marble. It was the first item on Napoleon's list of treasures that he wanted to take back to France after conquering Britain. He didn't quite make it!

Nearly one million nails, each hand-made, were buried by the Romans at a fortress near Dunkeld on the River Tay. They had to abandon the fort and did not want the precious iron to fall into enemy hands. If it had been found by the Celts, they would have had the nails remade into swords and spears.

The Celtic people loved decoration and ornament. When the Romans entered Strathclyde they were met by 300 Celtic chiefs wearing torcs of pure gold around their necks. These torcs were made from gold that had been collected from the streams that flowed into the River Clyde.

Julius Caesar was a keen collector of pearls. He would sometimes weigh them in the palm of his hand to judge their value. The pearls from Britain were highly valued and of good quality.

An enthusiastic amateur archaeologist may have discovered the most northerly amphitheatre in the Roman Empire at Newstead, near Melrose.

The Romans were excellent land surveyors. A series of watch-towers across Tayside controlled the movement of local people. There would have been a signalling system with beacon fires or smoke between watch-towers and the nearest fort. The watch-tower at Fendoch looks over the Sma' Glen and north towards the mountains of the Highlands. The legions were always prepared for trouble brewing from the north!

Crowds of over 3000 could have gathered at the Trimontium Theatre to watch bear-baiting, executions and military parades.

On the Lookout

What different signalling systems are used by these people today?

police
coastguards
fire service
lifeboat crews
infantry
breakdown
motoring service
air traffic control
ambulance

How many can you draw?

23

# EATING – ROMAN STYLE

In the army each eight-man squad organised its own cooking. Grain was stored in the fort granaries, which held supplies for a year at a time. Each unit ground their own corn ration into flour by turning two stones together. On the march, a legionary carried enough grain for about a fortnight, as well as a cooking pot, armour and weapons.

Soldiers cooked for their own unit and ate in their barrack rooms. The basics were provided by the army – corn, sour wine, meat and oil for cooking. The food was cooked in pots and pans over open fires. Basic foodstuffs were added to by buying any local produce, or by food parcels from home! Some food was brought in by road and by ship from the south.

Beef was a popular meat dish, but venison, small birds, chickens, milk, cheese and eggs, fish, shellfish and oysters were also eaten. Local vegetables and imported fruit added to the diet, but long Scottish winters on duty at the wall probably meant quite a boring diet for the soldiers during the colder months.

*How many of these fruits, herbs and vegetables which the Romans introduced to us can you identify?*

*(Answers on page 40.)*

Many plants were introduced to this country for the first time by the Romans. Herbs such as mint, parsley, thyme and bayleaf were much used in their cooking. It is said that the Romans fed garlic to their soldiers so they would fight better! In Bearsden, the seeds of coriander and opium poppy have been found, which were used for flavouring. Honey was used for sweetening foods and wine.

Keeping food fresh was a constant problem. Food often went rancid and a strong sauce was used to disguise the taste. The most popular sauce was made from fish, salt water and anchovies. Fresh meat in the winter was sometimes provided by keeping dormice in small clay pots. They were fattened up before they went into hibernation and then used as needed.

The variety of foodstuffs available meant that the soldiers in Scotland were adequately fed. Their staple daily diet would have had special feast days with more exotic foods, just as we have today.

*Bread was baked in ovens set into the back of a fort's ramparts. A fire was built in the oven to heat it, the ashes raked out and then the bread or meat baked or cooked inside it.*

Rotary Quern

Mortarium

*A mortarium was a bowl used for grinding and mixing food.*

*Rotary querns were made of two hard stones with a wooden handle and a turning piece in the centre. Querns found at Newstead were made from lava from the Rhineland. Even the Emperor Hadrian was known to grind his own corn ration when on active service.*

A Roman kettle on a grid iron which was put over an open fire, found at Trimontium, near Newstead.

Edible dormouse

# Health

In Roman times men could expect to live for around 60 years and women a few years less. Those who survived into their 70s or 80s were unusual. It is not until this century that because of better health care most people reach age 70 and beyond.

Larger forts had their own hospitals with medical staff for the army that included doctors, bandagers and orderlies. The doctors were often Greeks, who were more skilful at surgery and in the treatment of wounds.

Early Roman medicine was based on the use of herbs. It was also a mixture of science and religion. They learned a lot from the Greeks on the causes of disease. Common diseases for them were malaria, typhus, dysentery, tuberculosis, smallpox, anthrax, rabies and tetanus. There were no anaesthetics or antibiotics. Surgery was by trial and error. But they were able to make artificial limbs and teeth. (Wealthy Romans could buy false teeth made from ivory.)

Some of the plants introduced by the Romans were also grown for use as medicines. Mustard and basil were good for the stomach; lemon balm for headaches; sage for sore throats; and for the soldiers on the wall – hot mashed turnips were applied to chilblains!

Surgical instr

As the Romans said:
'Mens sana in
corpore sano.'
(A healthy mind
in a healthy body.)

Many medical words which we use today come from Latin. Try to find these 12 words in the wordsearch. (Answers on page 40)

| | |
|---|---|
| ambulance | *ambulare*, to walk |
| amputate | *amputare*, to cut off |
| casualty | *casus*, chance, fall |
| consultant | *consultare*, to consult |
| doctor | *doctus*, skilled |
| fracture | *frangere*, to break |
| hospital | *hospitium*, guest-house |
| infirmary | *infirmus*, weak |
| invalid | *invalidus*, weak |
| medicine | *medicus*, doctor |
| operation | *opera*, work |
| patient | *patiens*, suffering |

...nts used by a Roman doctor

# THE BATH-HOUSE

Each fort had a bath-house, built outside the ramparts because of the risk of fire. Within the bath block was a changing room, then a number of steam rooms at various temperatures for hot and cold baths. The sweating room was like a sauna with dry heat.

After rubbing themselves down with oil the soldiers moved through a series of rooms of increasing temperature to open the pores of their skin. They could then remove the oil and dirt with a special scraper, called a *strigil*. A dip in the cold plunge-bath then closed the pores and prevented the soldiers from catching cold.

The warm and hot rooms in the bath-house were heated by hypocaust – like underfloor central heating. Large blocks of stone were heated up by

*A soldier scraping off oil with a strigil*

*Furnace*

*A hypocaust system.*

28

the furnace and kept their heat long after the fire had died down. Hot air circulated under the floor and up the walls, providing most of the heat.

For off-duty soldiers the bath-house was a meeting place where they could keep warm, exchange news and gamble. Even a trip to the toilet was sociable! The dirty water from the bath-house was used to flush the toilets. Instead of loo paper, sponges or lumps of moss on sticks were used.

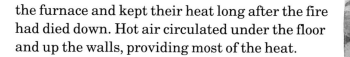

*Soldiers at the toilet*

*Soldiers gambling at a gaming table. Roman soldiers liked gambling and made their own counters for board games from pieces of tile, pottery or shale. They also enjoyed playing at marbles and dice.*

*Roman dice were either 6 or 12 sided. They were either marked with dots or with Roman numerals.*

Make a 12 sided dice using this pentagon shape as a guide

# CALCULATING – ROMAN STYLE

## Counting

Counting in tens, because of the ten fingers of our two hands, has been in use for thousands of years. Merchants throughout the Roman Empire who traded with others – whose language was different – showed numbers by their fingers.

Roman numbers were made up from letters. It was easy to add and subtract Roman numerals, but much more difficult to multiply and divide. Since about AD 1500 Roman numerals have been replaced by Arabic numbers. You can still see Roman numerals in use on clocks, watches, milestones, gravestones and TV credits at the end of a programme.

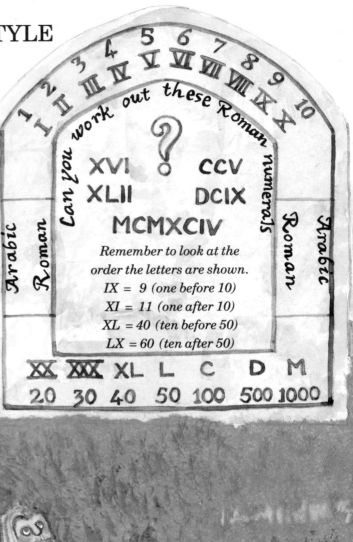

Can you work out these Roman numerals

XVI    CCV
XLII    DCIX
MCMXCIV

Remember to look at the order the letters are shown.

IX = 9 (one before 10)
XI = 11 (one after 10)
XL = 40 (ten before 50)
LX = 60 (ten after 50)

XX   XXX   XL   L   C   D   M
20   30   40   50   100   500   1000

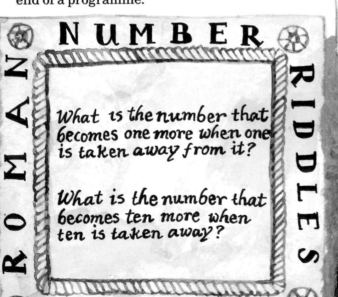

# ROMAN NUMBER RIDDLES

What is the number that becomes one more when one is taken away from it?

What is the number that becomes ten more when ten is taken away?

Answers on page 40

For speedier calculations some merchants used an abacus, not unlike our calculator of today. Others used pebbles and lined them up in tens and units to speed up their adding. ( The Latin word *calculus* means pebble.)

## Measuring

Measuring distance was important to the Romans for their roads and wall building. As the Latin for 1000 is *mille*, the distance a soldier could go in 1000 paces became known as a mile. A pace was in fact two strides and the Roman mile was about 1618 yards (1475 metres).

The stone slabs along the Antonine Wall record the length of wall completed by each legion.

*For the Emperor Caesar Titus Aelius Antoninus Pius, Father of his Country, a detachment of the Twentieth Valerian and Victorious Legion completed (the wall) over a distance of 3000 paces.*

*The Twentieth Valerian and Victorious Legion completed 3600 paces.*

# The Latin Alphabet and Language

Although the Romans occupied Britain for hundreds of years, Latin never became the national language. The Celts would only have learned short Latin words that were easy to pronounce and remember, connected with their trading, travel and food. When the Roman troops withdrew, the Celts carried on with their native language, but some Latin words remained in use.

Yet despite this, the Latin language was understood throughout the Empire and was the official language of the Church and State for centuries. Latin became an international language for science and scholarship. It provided terms for law and medicine in use today; and plants are still classified with Latin names.

So the Latin language, although no longer spoken, lives on, and our present English language has been enriched by it.

*The Romans were skilled at sending secret messages by code. Caesar's alphabet was one way used by the Roman Emperor Julius Caesar. The normal alphabet was written out and underneath it the alphabet was written out again – but this time beginning with the letter D. (To avoid confusion the full alphabet has been used here!)*

*A B C D E F G H I J K L M N O P Q R S T U V W X Y Z*

*D E F G H I J K L M N O P Q R S T U V W X Y Z A B C*

*It was this second alphabet which was used to code messages. So if Caesar wanted to send the message INVADE BRITAIN, I becomes L, N becomes Q and so on. The whole message would then read  LQUDGH EULWDLQ.*

*Now try to decode this secret message sent from the frontline!*

*ZLQWHU HQGOHVV LQ FDOHGRQLD. VHQG PRUH VXSSOLHU.*

NEMO ME IMPUNE LACESSIT!

VENI • VIDI • VICI

The motto of Scotland is "Nemo me impune lacessit" In Scots this means: "Wha daur meddle wi' me?" or in English: "No one provokes me with impunity!"

family, and if your school or town has a motto. Write them down and try to work out the meaning

Nil Desperandum = 'Don't give up'

# THE LATIN ALPHABET AND LANGUAGE

The Latin alphabet was used throughout the Roman Empire. It had only 23 letters.

Which ones are missing?

During the Middle Ages the Roman I was divided into i and j; and their v became u, v and w.

The Latin Alphabet

The English Alphabet

# ROMAN TECHNOLOGY

## Roads

When they were not fighting the Roman Legions acted as pioneers. They built forts, bridges and roads. They planned and built with such skill that after they left Britain their roads continued as the main routes for centuries. In Scotland, Dere Street is the basis of much of the present route of the A68.

Roads were usually built in a straight line

Routes were worked out using a groma.

Using three sides of a large box try designing a diorama of a Roman road with Roman soldiers on the march.

You've probably heard about Roman roads.....

## Weapons

The Roman army designed large weapons for use on a battlefield or in a siege. The simplest was the battering ram used to break down gates of a town or fort. The *onager* or catapult could fire huge stones a long distance. A *ballista* was a small field-gun which fired arrows or bolts.

ballista

onager

## Book-making

Wooden writing tablets were used in large numbers by the Roman army to record orders and deliveries of supplies. They wrote in ink on tablets of wood and joined them together like a concertina. They opened out in order just like unfolding a computer print-out.

# TRANSPORT AND TRADE

Traders had a busy time around the Roman forts bartering or selling food, animals and cloth. Trade with the rest of the empire was also important. Luxury goods such as wine and fruit, glass and high-quality pottery were imported – often solely for officer use. Officers and centurions enjoyed a much higher standard of living. They preferred crockery of glossy Samian ware made in France, together with glass and bronze vessels.

The food imported was contained in amphorae of different shapes according to the contents, or from which country they came. The carrot-shaped amphorae came from the Mediterranean and may have contained beans, lentils, honey, salted fish, dried fruit, cherries, plums, figs and dates.

Most amphorae found in Scotland came from around Seville and Córdoba in the south of Spain. They were shipped to Marseilles in the south of France, taken by boat northwards up the River Rhône, down the River Rhine by barge and across the Channel to Britain. And all of this happened before our present-day Common Market!

Food supplies to garrisons were taken in long columns of ox- or horse-drawn carts and wagons, using the great road system of the empire. These same carts also carried gravel for surfacing roads, building stone from quarries or military equipment – they were multi-purpose vehicles!

Large quantities of supplies were brought north to Scotland by merchant ships. Harbours at Inveresk and Cramond on the Forth, Carpow on the Tay and Irvine on the Clyde had roads linking up with the forts.

Many amphorae have been discovered in ancient shipwrecks. Paint your own shipwreck, with amphorae of different kinds on the sea bed. Now add interesting underwater detail with strands of wool or thin strips of paper for seaweed.

Today's Specials
Ham from Gaul
Figs from Spain
Cheeses from Gaul
Honey from Greece

FISH SAUCE

FRANCE

WINE

SPAIN

SWEET DRINK

ITALY

WINE

SPAIN

OLIVE OIL

# The Legacy of Rome

Roman troops were officially withdrawn from Britain in AD 410 to defend Italy from attack. However, through the centuries much of their way of life has survived. There are many features of our daily life which the Romans gave to us and we now take for granted. These are some of them.

## Buildings

*The Romans set a great example of how to build with fine stonework. Many of our public buildings look like Roman temples. They were also first to use concrete. Archaeologists have found Roman mortar so hard after 2000 years that their drills go through surrounding rock more easily than through the mortar!*

*Roman architects were excellent engineers. They were the first to use the arch for bridge-building. Their designs have never been bettered and were copied by 19th-century railway engineers for their viaducts. We have also inherited glass windows and central heating from the Romans.*

## Coinage and Banking

*Coins were originally minted to pay soldiers' wages and to make the collection of taxes easier.*

*We use £ to stand for one pound of our money, from Libra – a pound in weight. Our pound sterling used to be a pound weight in silver.*

| M | H | S | M | I | H | I | V | T | B | K | Z | O | D |
|---|---|---|---|---|---|---|---|---|---|---|---|---|---|
| V | Y | R | Y | S | N | Q | N | F | H | X | P | X | E |
| H | O | Z | J | T | O | P | G | Y | D | S | S | M | O |
| D | V | C | O | A | S | R | E | V | E | C | I | V | G |
| A | I | T | A | R | G | I | L | P | M | E | X | E | R |
| N | O | T | A | B | E | N | E | M | F | J | T | F | A |
| M | A | G | N | U | M | O | P | U | S | H | A | M | T |
| A | N | T | E | M | E | R | I | D | I | E | M | M | I |
| B | O | N | A | F | I | D | E | G | B | H | S | Q | A |
| P | S | I | T | N | E | M | S | O | P | M | O | C | S |

## Latin Language

*We still use many Latin words and phrases. How many of these do you know? Can you find them in the wordsearch?*

ante meridiem (am) = *before noon*
bona fide = *in good faith, genuine*
compos mentis = *of sound mind*
Deo gratias = *thanks to God*
exempli gratia (eg) = *for example*
in toto = *entirely*
magnum opus = *a great work*
nota bene (NB) = *note well*
vice versa = *the other way round*

## Roman Numerals

*Clocks and watches often have Roman numerals on them. What does it say under this clockface?*
*(Answer on page 40)*

## Planets

*The planets in our solar system are named after Roman gods and goddesses.*

## The Calendar

*The Roman year originally had only 10 months. September was the seventh month through to December – the tenth month. Julius Caesar reformed the calendar. His scientists calculated that the solar year lasted 365 ¼ days. Every fourth year was to have an extra day added. The fifth month was renamed July to honour Julius Caesar. Unfortunately those in charge got it wrong, until Emperor Augustus sorted it out. The sixth month was then renamed August to honour himself!*

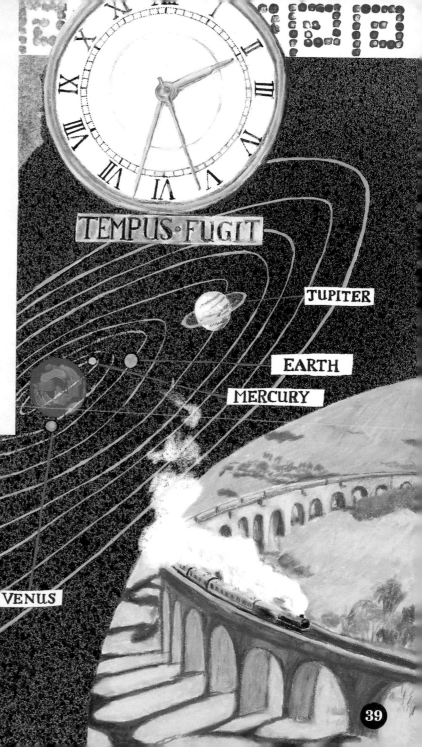

TEMPUS·FUGIT

JUPITER

EARTH

MERCURY

MARS

SATURN

NEPTUNE

VENUS

URANUS

PLUTO

# PLACES TO VISIT/ANSWERS

**Trimontium**
Trimontium Exhibition,
Ormiston Institute,
The Square, **Melrose**
Tel 089682 2463
Exhibition based on the finds from the Roman
army's headquarters in Scotland. Also a
yearly update of the current excavations at
Trimontium.

**Hadrian's Wall**
Roman Army Museum (part of Hadrian's
Wall World Heritage Site) Carvoran,
Greenhead, **Northumberland**
Tel 06977 47485
Reconstructions of Roman life in sight and
sound. Their aim is to make Roman frontier
history 'come alive'.

**Vindolanda,** The Vindolanda Trust,
Chesterholm Museum, Bardon Mill, Hexham,
**Northumberland**
Tel 0434 344277
Excavation sites of 15 acres. Listening posts:
Corinthus describes life as a soldier on the
frontier. Full-scale reconstructions of sections
of Hadrian's Wall. Museum and film theatre.

**Stories about Romans in Britain**
*The Eagle of the Ninth; The Silver Brand;
Song for a Dark Queen; The Lantern Bearers;
Frontier Wolf* by Rosemary Sutcliff
*Legions of the Eagle* by Henry Treece

**Page 5: Spot the wild boar**
There are 9 wild boars throughout the book.
inside front cover - 1 boar
- page 5 - 3 boars
- page 6 - 1 boar (on flag)
- page 18 - 2 boars
- page 31 - 1 boar
- this page - 1 boar

**Page 10: Odd words out** = trip, trigger,
trifle (triangle, tripod, tricycle, trio, trilogy,
trinity, tricolour, triplets = 3 of something)

**Page 13: Check your atlas**
Oceanus Atlanticus = Atlantic Ocean
Oceanus Hibernicus = Irish Sea
Oceanus Germanicus = North Sea

**Page 17: Roman Gods and Goddesses**
(from left to right)
1 Bacchus = god of wine
2 Vesta = goddess of the hearth
3 Jupiter = god of the weather
4 Diana = goddess of the moon and hunting
5 Mithras = god of light
6 Janus = god of beginnings

**Page 19: Bridgeness Slab**
The three animals being sacrificed at the
altar are: a pig (sus), a sheep (ovis) and a bull
(taurus). Their sacrifice was part of the ritual
cleansing of the legion.

**Page 24: Fruits, herbs and vegetables
introduced by the Romans**
apples, plums, cherries, beans, celery, peas,
parsley, radish, fennel, pepper, dill.

**Page 27: Medical Wordsearch**

| I | N | V | A | L | I | D | C | E | T | I | M | O | B |
|---|---|---|---|---|---|---|---|---|---|---|---|---|---|
| C | P | P | R | J | F | A | C | H | N | N | E | P | G |
| D | O | C | T | O | R | N | A | O | A | F | D | E | T |
| R | Q | E | F | I | Z | S | S | T | I | I | R | N |   |
| V | U | E | T | L | C | Y | U | P | L | R | C | A | E |
| Q | O | P | U | E | T | F | A | I | U | M | I | T |   |
| L | V | B | O | W | U | A | L | T | S | A | N | I | T |
| B | M | A | U | J | R | Y | T | A | N | R | E | O | A |
| A | O | T | L | O | E | K | Y | L | O | Y | Q | N | P |
| E | T | A | T | U | P | M | A | K | C | M | E | X | S |

**Page 30: Roman number riddles**
XVI = 16
XLII = 42
CCV = 205
DCIX = 609
MCMXCIV = 1994

What is the number that becomes
one more when one is taken away from it? IX
What is the number that becomes 10 more
when 10 is taken away? XL

**Page 32: Caesar's code**
WINTER/ ENDLESS/ IN/
CALEDONIA/ SEND/ MORE /
SUPPLIES

**Page 38: Latin language wordsearch**

| M | H | S | M | I | H | V | T | B | K | Z | O | D |
|---|---|---|---|---|---|---|---|---|---|---|---|---|
| V | Y | R | Y | S | Q | N | F | H | X | P | X | E |
| H | O | Z | J | T | O | P | G | Y | D | S | S | M | O |
| D | V | C | O | A | S | R | E | V | E | C | I | V | G |
| A | I | Z | A | R | G | I | L | P | M | E | X | E | R |
| N | O | T | A | B | E | N | E | M | F | J | T | F | A |
| M | A | G | N | U | M | O | P | U | S | H | A | M | T |
| A | N | T | E | M | E | R | I | D | I | E | M | M | I |
| B | O | N | A | F | I | D | E | G | B | H | S | Q | A |
| P | S | I | T | N | E | M | S | O | P | M | O | C | S |

**Page 39: Tempus fugit** = Time flies